8/13

CR

GALLUP GUIDES FOR YOUTH FACING PERSISTENT PREJUDICE

Native North American Indians

GALLUP GUIDES FOR YOUTH FACING PERSISTENT PREJUDICE

- Asians
- Blacks
- Hispanics
- Jews
- The LGBT Community
- Muslims
- Native North American Indians
- People with Mental and Physical Challenges

GALLUP GUIDES FOR YOUTH FACING PERSISTENT PREJUDICE

Native North American Indians

Ellyn Sanna

Mason Crest

Mason Crest
370 Reed Road
Broomall, Pennsylvania 19008
www.masoncrest.com

Printed and bound in the United States of America.

First printing
9 8 7 6 5 4 3 2 1

ISBN-13: 978-1-4222-2462-5 (hardcover series)
ISBN-13: 978-1-4222-2469-4 (hardcover)
ISBN-13: 978-1-4222-9342-3 (e-book)
ISBN-13: 978-1-4222-2478-6 (paperback)

Cataloging-in-Publication Data on file with Library of Congress.

Sanna, Ellyn, 1957-
 Native North American Indians / by Ellyn Sanna.
     p. cm. -- (Gallup guides for youth facing persistent prejudice)
 Includes bibliographical references and index.
  ISBN 978-1-4222-2469-4 (hardcover) -- ISBN 978-1-4222-2462-5 (series hardcover) -- ISBN 978-1-4222-2478-6 (pbk.) -- ISBN 978-1-4222-9342-3 (ebook)
 1. Indians of North America--History--Juvenile literature. 2. Indians of North America--Social conditions--Juvenile literature. 3. Indians of North America--Crimes against--Juvenile literature. 4. Race discrimination--United States--Juvenile literature. 5. United States--Race relations--Juvenile literature. 6. India I. Title.
 E77.4.S26 2012
 970.004'97--dc23
                                            2012021142

Produced by Harding House Publishing Services, Inc.
www.hardinghousepages.com
Interior design by Micaela Sanna.
Page design elements by Cienpies Design / Illustrations | Dreamstime.com.
Cover design by Torque Advertising + Design.

With thanks to Lawrence Jackson and Hunter RedDay for their help with this book. Special thanks also to Lauren Wilsey for her photography.

CONTENTS

Prejudice and Natives

"When you have nothing," says Hunter RedDay, "you resent people who look like they have everything."

Hunter is a punk musician—and he's also a Native American. His mother is Diné (what many white people refer to as Navajo), and his father is Sioux. His aunts are married to Blackfoot men, so Hunter has connections to several tribal groups. He's thought a lot about prejudice and the ways it has affected people he knows.

Prejudice is a two-way street, Hunter believes. It's something **minorities** experience—"But then they turn it around and send it right back," he says. "Envy and jealousy turn into hatred. They turn into racism. When your only choices out on the Rez are death or jail, all you have to call your own is your desperation. You're a captive, and racism is your cell. It keeps you in—and it keeps everyone else out. You're like an abandoned building, something that's empty and useless. You're not really alive anymore. All you've got is rage, but you

High School Stereotypes

The average high school has its share of stereotypes—lumping a certain kind of person together, ignoring all the ways that each person is unique. These stereotypes are often expressed with a single word or phrase: "jock," "nerd," "goth," "prep," or "geek." The images these words call to mind are easily recognized and understood by others. But that doesn't mean they're true!

Different Names

When Columbus saw the people who lived in the Americas, he named them "Indians," since he wrongly believed he was in the outer reaches of India. The word stuck. It became one of the categories in our heads, another comprehensive stereotype where we could file in a single slot what are actually many different groups of people. To this day, Native people of the Americas are often called "Indians" in the English-speaking world, or "Indios" in Spanish. Today, many Native people prefer to identify themselves by the name of their individual tribes: Cherokee, Zuni, Houma, Diné, and so on.

The term "Native American" is an alternative name that is used in the United States today, while many Canadians use the terms "First Nations," "Aboriginal people," and "Indigenous people" to refer to the same large group of people.

don't do anything with it, you don't use it to create anything new. You're not evolving, you're not growing."

Hunter shakes his head, and he looks sad. "Prejudice is a monster you can't really kill. It's just part of the human experience—like lice and old age. It's part of the load you have to accept when you're human."

WHAT IS PREJUDICE?

The root word of prejudice is "pre-judge." Prejudiced people often judge others based purely on their race or ethnic group;

The word "Native" is used to refer to the people who lived in the Americas before Europeans arrived (as well as to their descendants who still live in the Americas today). Many groups of many different people, with many languages and many cultures, actually lived in the Americas. To the Europeans, however, they looked like one single group.

they make assumptions about others that may have no basis in reality. They believe that if your skin is darker or you speak a different language or wear different clothes or worship God in a different way, then they already know you are not as smart, not as nice, not as honest, not as valuable, or not as moral as they are. Native Americans have been the victims of prejudice ever since white people came to North America.

Why do human beings experience prejudice? **Sociologists** believe humans have a basic tendency to fear anything that's unfamiliar or unknown. Someone who is strange (in that they're not like us) is scary; they're automatically dangerous or inferior. If we get to know the strangers, of course, we end up discovering that they're not so different from ourselves. They're not so frightening and threatening after all. But too often, we don't let that happen. We put up a wall between the strangers and ourselves. We're on the inside; they're on the outside. And then we peer over the wall, too far away from the people on the other side to see anything but our differences. That's what has often happened when people of other ethnicities interacted in the United States.

And here's where another human tendency comes into play: stereotyping.

STEREOTYPES

A stereotype is a fixed, commonly held idea or image of a person or group that's based on an **oversimplification** of some observed or imagined trait. Stereotypes assume that whatever is believed about a group is typical for each and every individual within that group. "Girls aren't good at math," is a stereotype. "White people can't dance," is another. "People who wear glasses are nerds," is yet another, and "All hairdressers are gay," is one as well.

Many stereotypes tend to make us feel superior in some way to the person or group we're stereotyping. Not all stereotypes are negative, however; some are positive—"Black men are good at basketball," "Gay guys have good fashion sense," or "Asian students are smart"—but that doesn't make them true. They ignore individuals' uniqueness. They make assumptions that may or may not be accurate.

We can't help our human tendency to put people into categories. Like Hunter said, it's part of being human. As babies, we faced a confusing world filled with an amazing variety of new things. We needed a way to make sense of it all, so one of our first steps in learning about the world around us was to sort things into separate slots in our heads: small furry things that said *meow* were kitties, while larger furry things that said *arf-arf* were doggies; cars went *vroom-vroom*, but trains were longer and went *choo-choo*; little girls looked one way and little boys another; and doctors wore white coats, while police

In the early twentieth century, photographer Edward S. Curtis took photos like this one of Native people living in the West. These photographs were respectful and beautiful—but they also reinforced a new stereotype in Americans' minds: that Native people were a noble, romantic, and dying culture, rather than living, breathing human beings with challenges and contributions that were both part of the United States.

Six Characteristics of a Racial Minority Group

1. Minority group members suffer oppression at the hands of another group.
2. A minority group is identified by certain traits that are clearly visible and obvious.
3. Minorities see themselves as belonging to a special and separate social unit; they identify with others like themselves.
4. A person does not voluntarily become a member of a minority; he or she is born into it.
5. Members of racial minority groups usually don't marry outside the group. If intermarriage is high, ethnic identities and loyalties are weakening.
6. "Minority" is a social, not a numerical concept. In other words, it doesn't matter how many members of a particular "out-group" live in a region compared to the "in-group"; what matters are who has the power and social prestige.

officers wore blue. These were our earliest stereotypes. They were a handy way to make sense of the world. They helped us know what to expect, so that each time we faced a new person or thing, we weren't starting all over again from scratch.

But stereotypes become dangerous when we continue to hold onto our mental images despite new evidence. Stereotypes are particularly dangerous and destructive when they're directed at persons or groups of persons. That's when they turn into prejudice.

"When you think you can reduce a human being to a single term," Hunter says, "when you can say, 'You're an Indian—and that's ALL you are'—that's racism."

RACISM

Prejudice and racism go hand-in-hand. Prejudice is an attitude, a way of looking at the world. When it turns into action it's called discrimination. Discrimination is when people are treated differently (and unfairly) because they belong to a particular group of people. Racism is a combination of the two. It's treating members of a certain "race" differently because you think they're not as good, simply because they belong to that race. You might say that prejudice is the root of racism— and discrimination is its branches and leaves.

Ethnocentrism

Ethnocentrism refers to a tendency to view one's own ethnic group's behaviors as "normal." Other groups are not only viewed as different, but they are seen as strange and sometimes inferior.

There's one other concept that's important to racism as well—the belief that human beings can be divided into groups that are truly separate and different from one another. Scientists aren't convinced this is really possible, though. Biologically, people are more alike than they're different, no matter what color their skin is or what continent their ancestors came from.

Native people are just as likely to be smart as anyone else. They are just as trustworthy and kind, just as moral and hardworking. Some Natives are alcoholics or abuse drugs—and so do some white people. Many Natives have problems. So do many whites.

Racism tells lies. Prejudice against Native people is one of those lies.

North American Native Groups

There are hundreds of different Native groups that live in North America. Here are just a few of the largest groups:

- Apache: Southwest United States
- Cherokee: Southeast United States
- Cree: Midwest United States and Canada
- Diné (Navajo): Southwest United States
- Inuit: Northern Canada and Alaska
- Iroquois: Northeast United States and Canada
- Mixtec: Mexico
- Nahuatl: Mexico
- Ojibwe: Great Lakes Region (U.S. and Canada)
- Pueblo: Southwest United States
- Seminoles: Southeast United States
- Sioux: Midwest United States
- Tlingit: Pacific Northwest (U.S. and Canada)
- Yucatec (Maya): Mexico

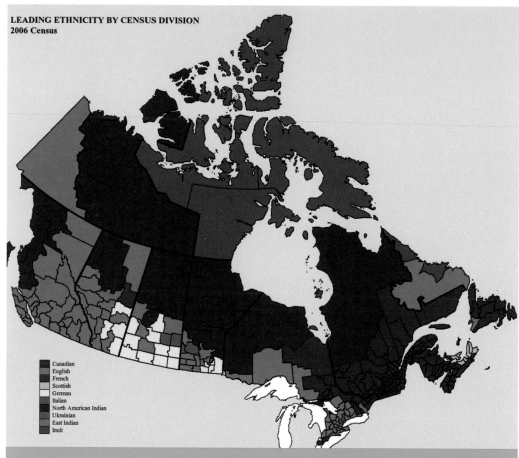

LEADING ETHNICITY BY CENSUS DIVISION
2006 Census

Canadian
English
French
Scottish
German
Italian
North American Indian
Ukrainian
East Indian
Inuit

In some areas of Canada, the Native population is greater than any other in that region. Areas of this map colored dark brown and bright purple are where most of the population is either "North American Indian" or "Inuit."

Native North American Indians

How Many Native North Americans?

According the U.S. 2006 Census, about .8 percent of the American population is Native. That's about 2.5 million people. However, Native people aren't spread out evenly across the United States. In Alaska, for instance, more than 13 percent of the population is Native, and in New Mexico and South Dakota about 9 percent of the population is Native. Meanwhile, in many states along the eastern seaboard, only .1 or .2 percent of the people are Native.

Meanwhile, Canada's population in the 2006 census was 3.75 percent Native (about 1.2 million people). As is the case in the United States, however, Native people aren't spread evenly across Canada. In fact, in many regions, there are more Natives than there are whites.

In Mexico, nearly 10 percent of the population is Native. That's nearly 10 million people. The largest numbers live in central and southern Mexican states, such as the Yucatan and Oaxaca.

History Lesson

If we could look down from outer space, we'd see that humanity inhabits a single enormous blue sphere—our Earth. If we divide this globe by cutting it in half from top to bottom, we can imagine hemispheres. ("Hemi" means half, and a sphere is round, so a hemisphere is half of something round, in this case, the globe.) The Eastern Hemisphere contains Africa, Australia, Europe, and Asia. People who come from this part of the world sometimes call it the "Old World." The Western Hemisphere consists of what we today call the "Americas." Once they became aware of it, people in the Eastern Hemisphere called the Western Hemisphere the

"New World." But it wasn't new to the millions of people who had lived there for thousands of years!

Who discovered this vast Western Hemisphere? Which direction did they come from? No one today knows. They came at least 15,000 years ago. Until recently, scientists felt certain people walked from Asia into North America over a

Archeological Controversy

Not all historians and archeologists agree that the land bridge theory is correct. Some of the most ancient yet most advanced prehistoric cultures have been found in the extreme south of South America. If migration went north to south, how did people get south first? Some scientists think early people may have arrived in South America by boat thousands of years before others migrated across Beringia. Stone tools found in South America appear to be at least 20,000 years old, older than any of the commonly accepted dates of North American sites. Several groups of Native people say they originated in the Americas. Maybe different groups of people arrived different ways. We may never be able to prove how, when, or why the first people came to the Americas.

This woman belongs to a Native group called the Huichol. They live in Zacatecas, Mexico.

land bridge that temporarily connected those continents—a narrow piece of land called Beringia between what is today Russia and Alaska. These early adventurers were hunters who dressed in warm skins and followed herds of mammoths for their food. According to this theory, they walked from north to south until they had spread out over all of North, Central, and South America.

When Europeans arrived, the Western Hemisphere was already home to hundreds of cultures, with a vast variety of languages, customs, and spiritual beliefs. Scholars estimate between 40 and 90 million people—the ancestors of the people we refer to as Natives—inhabited the Americas before Columbus arrived. Once Columbus stepped foot on the "New World," both worlds, old and new, would change forever.

This photograph taken in the 1940s makes clear that Native people weren't welcome to interact socially with whites in this bar.

After that first contact between the two hemispheres, Columbus recorded his thoughts in his private journal. The Natives would "become Christians very easily," he wrote, "for it seems they have no religion." He also noted they would "make good and intelligent slaves." He decided to take some of them back to Spain as captives.

From the beginning, Europeans saw the Native people as the fulfillment for their selfish wishes. Columbus regarded them as childlike, innocent people. He assumed they would willingly serve Spanish masters.

For the Natives of the Americas, this first contact with Europe was the beginning of a battle for cultural survival that continues today. Historians who study the horrific number of Native deaths that followed contact with Europe conclude that this may be history's worst case of **genocide**. No one knows for sure how many Native people died following Columbus's voyage, but an average estimate is around 40 million in the first hundred years. Although the European invaders murdered many of the Natives, many more died from diseases to which they had no **immunity**.

Caucasians had been in the Western Hemisphere before Columbus: the Vikings landed on the East Coast, and Irish monks may have visited the Americas. Yet their visits were just blips on the radar screen of history. After Columbus, for better or worse, the fates of Europe and the Americas were bound together.

Natives in Mexico

In most Latin American countries like Mexico (as well as the nations of Central and South America), Native people were not sent to reservations the way they were in the United States and Canada. The white people who settled Mexico came from Spain rather than England and France. They killed the Native people and took their land, and many Natives died from European diseases, just as they had to the north. However, the Spanish also intermarried with the Natives. This helped make the line between whites and Natives more blurry, less obvious.

Despite that, Native people in Mexico still experience prejudice. Prejudice toward "pureblood" Indians from those who are "mixed-blood" (Spanish and Indian) is all too common. People who are darker-skinned and of Native descent have fewer educational and job opportunities—and lighter-skinned, Spanish-descent Mexicans tend to be wealthier and better educated.

In the Americas, the Native people would face centuries of prejudice. In the United States, their land was taken from them, and they were rounded up and put on **reservations**, where they struggled to hold on to their culture despite poverty, alcoholism, and the loss of the natural environment on which their traditions depended. In Canada, Natives were given land referred to as reserves. Over the past twenty years, Canada has established a process by which Native groups can file claims for lost land. In some cases, the government has restored land to Native nations, and the Canadian territory of Nunavut belongs now to the Inuit people. Despite this, Canadian Native groups also continue to face prejudice and discrimination, just as they do in the United States.

Real-Life Stories

"Don't judge someone until you've walked a mile in his shoes," is an old proverb. It's actually a Native American saying. It means don't look down on anyone until you understand what it's like to be that person.

Obviously, we can never really know what's it like to live inside someone else's life—but the more we can learn from others' histories, the less likely we are to be prejudiced against entire groups of people. And the more we get to know the

This is the rough land that the Apache and Yavapai marched across back in 1875.

real-life stories of living, breathing Native people, the less we will think that all Native Americans are the same.

LARRY JACKSON

Larry Jackson lives on the Yavapai-Apache Reservation in Arizona. His mother was Hopi, his father was Apache, and his wife is Yavapai. His roots are deep in this area along Arizona's Verde River.

On February 27, 1875, the United States Army forced about 1,500 Yavapai and Apache people off from this same land along the Rio Verde. The entire community, including those who were sick, very young, and very old, was forced to march 180 miles overland to San Carlos, Arizona. They crossed mountains and flooded rivers during winter storms. Some drowned, and many fell ill. Hundreds of people died. Those who survived were **interred** on land that was far away from their homes.

Twenty-five years later, about two hundred Yavapai and Apache returned to the Verde Valley to the land that had been theirs. They found, however, that their land had been taken over by white settlers. There was next to nothing left for them. But the Yavapai and Apache refused to abandon their homeland again, and finally, in 1909, the U.S. government established a reservation for them there.

Although the group was made up of two different tribal groups, by this time they shared a common history. In 1934, when the U.S. government passed the Indian Reorganization Act, the Yavapai and Apache people became officially recognized as a **sovereign** people, the Yavapai-Apache Tribe. In 1992, the Yavapai-Apache people voted to revise their original constitution to reflect a new identity: they were now two tribes that had merged into the Yavapai-Apache Nation.

Today, everyone who lives on Larry's street is literally family. For him, "community" and "family" mean the same thing.

Larry didn't grow up here, though. His father was in the Army, and so Larry was born in Los Angeles. He spent his childhood in California, but when he was a teenager, he came to live with his grandmother in Arizona in a little wooden house by the Verde River, near the street where he still lives today. He met his wife here—and he embraced this corner of the world as home, the place where he would put down roots of his own.

Growing up, Larry didn't think much about prejudice. It wasn't something he ran into while he lived in California. Not until he came to Arizona did he understand that some people looked down on him because of his family heritage.

At the same time, he hasn't always been completely accepted by the people who live with him on the Yavapai-Apache Reservation. "My generation is a lost one," he says. "Our fathers went off the reservation to seek the advantages they could find away from the land that had always been ours. We were raised as non-Natives. Our parents spoke the old languages to each other, but not to us. We grew up as Americans, rather than Natives." Like his father, Larry joined the Army and served for twenty years. He came back home to the Yavapai-Apache Reservation in 2001, where he then became a pastor and a tutor to his community's children. Especially at first, he found that his peers in the community often didn't regard him as being truly one of them. He hadn't grown up there, and he had been away for years. "Being Native is more than just your ancestry," he says. "It's also a lifestyle. It's who you are as an individual."

For Larry, the small community where he lives is essential to his identity today. "I do not think of myself as a Native American. Instead, I am a part of a tribal community. Here we embrace the identity of who we are. We don't understand why we have to be identified with a larger group. Why do we have to be called Native Americans? Why can't we be simply the Yavapai-Apache?"

During his years in the Army, Larry never settled down in one place. "But through all my travels, I knew I would come home to this land. This home is more important to me than money."

Larry Jackson lives here in this small community on the Yavapai-Apache Reservation. Nearly everyone on his street is related to him in some way.

Native North American Indians

Larry also feels a deep connection to his Hopi roots. When his mother was dying, Larry went to her and asked her to give him a name. Since a person's uncles are the ones who have to give a Hopi name, and his mother had no brothers, Larry had to be adopted into another family before he could receive his name. Then his hair was washed and he took a name that tied him to his mother's people. "That's enough," he says. "Now my home and identity are complete."

As a veteran, however, Larry sometimes feels conflicted between different parts of his identity. He is both a loyal American and deeply committed to his tribal community. This conflict became obvious recently at a community celebration called Exodus, an annual **commemoration** of the time when the Yavapai-Apache were forced off their land by the American government. The veterans in the community, including Larry, were going to take part in the symbolic march—but other Yavapai-Apache protested that they didn't want the colors of the United States to be a part of the ceremony, since it was those same colors that had driven them off their land. In the end, Larry did not take part in the march at all.

The topic of prejudice makes Larry uncomfortable. "Native Americans are different from whites," he says. "We are who we are. We don't necessarily want to be accepted by whites. We acknowledge that everyone else is who they are as well. Why get so worked up about it?"

Focusing on prejudice, Larry says, puts people into groups, rather than looking at them as individuals. "Talking about prejudice," he says, "does the very thing that it claims to want to avoid—it looks at people in a larger context, as though they can be reduced to a category, rather than as individuals. That larger context isn't even accurate. When I was in the Army, everyone assumed I represented Native Americans as a whole. But Native Americans are not a **homogeneous** group. We are all different. We come from different backgrounds."

Personally, Larry feels called to be a peacemaker, and he strives to simply accept his identity. "As a Native person, I accept the world for what it is," he says. "I do not strive against it. I do not need to know everything, as a non-Native would. I do not need to control everything, as a white person would. The fruit of this acceptance is that I can be at peace with where I am. This covers the entire spectrum of my social life. The loving community where I live is enough for me. I am a part of creation. That is enough! I have accepted the limits of who I am. I identify with who I am."

And yet Larry refuses to sit back and do nothing when he sees racism hurt the children in his community. "Protecting our children is the line I have to draw between acceptance and becoming **proactive**," he says. "We must—we will!—protect our children and their future."

This is why Larry decided to become a tutor in the public school. "Our children are not accepted in the public schools where they attend. Our culture is not valued or protected there. There are no Natives on the faculty. The schools do not understand our traditional values. We are regarded as 'irresponsible parents.' Our children are expected to perform badly. They run into discipline problems that are the results of the miscommunications between cultures."

The public schools do not understand the values Native parents teach their children, Larry says. While non-Native children are taught to compete, to excel, to be independent, to achieve, and to accumulate material things, the children in Larry's community are taught just the opposite. "We see those values as a threat to the morals we want our children to have," he says. "Our children are taught to cooperate, to work together for the community. They are taught that material things are not 'mine' or 'yours.' Our houses, our land belong to

Real-Life Stories

us all. They don't belong to any single individual. For example, I couldn't go to the bank and take out a loan on my home, because it belongs to the tribe, not to me personally. We want our children to work for this community. We want them to grow up knowing they are totally loved and completely accepted here. They do not need to achieve anything to earn that love. They do not need to behave in a certain way to be accepted."

As a tutor in the public schools, Larry works to be an **advocate** for his community's children. It's not an easy role. He describes an incident where a couple of girls from the community got in trouble at school. The school demanded that the girls make a public apology at a school assembly, in front of the entire student body and faculty. The girls were understandably embarrassed and angry, and the public apology turned into a confrontation between the girls and the teachers. The girls were trying to defend themselves—but the teachers took it personally, as an insult to their authority. Afterward, the dean of students made it clear to the entire school that he considered these girls to be "hoodlums." Larry went to the superintendent on the girls' behalf, and the dean eventually apologized. "After that incident, however," Larry says, "my relationship with the faculty changed. They looked at me differently. I was no longer one of them. I was a Native in their eyes now, not another professional."

HUNTER REDDAY

Hunter was born in Tuba City, Arizona, but he spent his childhood in Utah. "I didn't hang out with Native kids much,"

Hunter is proud of his Native heritage—but he also feels enriched by black culture, especially the Rasta culture from Jamaica. "Our stories are the same," he says.

he says. "I didn't really know any First Nation kids my own age. My friends were white kids, black kids." He spoke Diné inside his house—"But outside, it was just grab your skateboard and go!"

Some of the kids he knew ended up joining gangs. But Hunter wasn't tempted. "I was different because I had my tribe, the people I came from. I knew who I was. I could say, 'This is where I belong. This is who I am.' I didn't need a gang to tell me that. I think gangs are just a way to make your own tribe, a group where you can belong when you don't belong anywhere else."

Then, when Hunter was a teenager, he came back to Tuba City. He had the good fortune to attend a wonderful school there. "That school made all the difference in who I am today," he says. "It taught me that there was another way besides racism. It taught me to be a human being first, before I was Hopi or Diné."

The school had a great creative program that allowed Hunter to write, compose music, go to museums and symphonies. He soon realized that music was his passion. "I had this teacher, a real **mentor**," he says. "He was a big black guy with Rasta dreds—his wife was a Hopi—and he just squashed prejudice in his students like it was a bug. He taught me that music belongs to us all. It's a channel for us all."

Hunter RedDay knows who he is—and he uses all his gifts to work for change in the world around him.

Hunter believes that living close to the land in Arizona has changed how he looks at life. "The Earth is a good teacher," he says.

Prejudice exists even between tribal groups, Hunter acknowledges. "There are lots of bad feelings between the Hopi and the Diné. But music makes a bridge. It's the universal language. It's a way to claim your own essence, your own story, your love—and then give it back to the world."

Native North American Indians

Hunter's **optimism** and **passion** shine in everything he says. But at the same time, he knows that prejudice is all too real. "America was built on blood," he says. "Racism—prejudice—it killed people. We like to hide that blood under the rug where we don't have to look at it. But it's still there. And we've added on centuries of racism and **elitism**, ugly stuff that trickles down from the higher levels—from the government, the media, the big corporations—and then runs into any little gaps it finds lower down, in people's minds, in their daily lives."

Hunter shakes his head. "Sometimes, prejudice isn't so much about the color of your skin. America doesn't worry so much as you might think about red or brown or black or white. The only color America really cares about is green. Whatever pumps the city. Whatever will make people rich, keep them rich, make them richer. Just happens that it's the white guys that are rich. And the poor people are just **commodities**. The people of color end up in the ghetto and on the Rez—while the white guys drive their big cars and live in their big houses."

Hunter acknowledges that it's easy to get angry when you're growing up poor without opportunities; it's easy to keep the cycle of hate and hopelessness turning around and around.

"When you grow up surrounded by concrete," he says, "when you grow up away from the Earth, it's easy to forget what you really know inside your heart. It's easy to lose who you are, to let it be stolen from you by the corporations and the media. All you start to see is closed doors in front of you—and behind you, this history of blood and racism."

"When you see the light, it's calling your name," Hunter says. "You just gotta learn to listen." The beauty of the Arizona land inspires him.

For Hunter, music is what showed him how to get past anger and prejudice. "It was punk," he says, "that got me back into my own **traditions**, my own **culture**. Punk was fast and furious—like the world out there—but it also sang about love and hope. Punk and hip-hop assaults your mind. It's not just a groove. It makes you question."

Rage Against the Machine was the group that first got Hunter thinking about the power of music. "That was it for me, that was my first," he says. "They're not just entertaining. They're exploding mind bombs! They taught me that it's not about destruction, though. It's about asking the questions that have to be asked—and then moving on. Keep going till you get to forgiveness."

Racism and prejudice became Hunter's musical inspiration. "That's what sets me on fire," he says. "Hatred . . . racism . . . they're my biggest inspirations. They give me a target to shoot toward. They're the fuel that I burn. I take all the anger, the rage, the injustice—and I transform it. I turn it into creativity."

Hunter refuses to let prejudice define him. "Prejudice and racism—they're just a waste of time, a waste of mental space," he says. "I've found myself. I know who I am, and I know what I'm going to do. I'm the right person in the right place. I keep looking at the light—I don't let myself focus on the darkness."

Fighting Prejudice

"We're all part of the game," says Hunter RedDay. "Racism and prejudice have made the rules—and all of us just keep on playing the same game, not even realizing what we're doing. Sometimes it's not the system 'out there' that's the problem. It's what's in here." He points to his own chest. "I learned that the battle I was fighting was in myself. It was in my home, in my own backyard."

So how do we fight this battle?

FORGIVENESS

Hunter believes that the first step is to forgive the past. "People have done horrible things to each other," he says. "White people killed the First Nations. First Nation people killed white people sometimes. Sometimes different tribes killed each other. And we all hang on to these things our ancestors did, as though those things happened to us personally. We can't forget the past. We can't forgive."

But we don't need to let the past define the present. "Our ancestors did terrible stuff," he acknowledges. "Your ancestors. My ancestors. But that's history. That's their story. It's our time now. What will the historians have to say about us? It's time to write a new story. This is a new chapter. And it's up to us to write it."

FOCUS ON THE INDIVIDUAL

Larry Jackson has his own perspective on how to fight prejudice, one that's a little different from Hunter's. "Words like 'racism' and 'prejudice,'" Larry says, "these are not constructive words. We can try to outlaw hatred, but we'll never be successful. When we focus on words like 'racism' and 'prejudice,' we're looking at the situation from a legal perspective rather than a personal one."

That's why Larry believes it's not productive to focus on groups of people—Native Americans, black Americans, Hispanic Americans, for example—rather than on individual human beings. "By making the leap into another situation—by making a conflict be between cultures instead of two people, by defining it as racism or prejudice, we just make the situation worse. We make the conflict seem bigger than it really is. We add on years of history and bad feelings to it. The bad feelings just grow."

Larry Jackson believes he is called to be a peacemaker. He tries to ease conflicts between individuals, rather than focusing on the issues between larger groups.

Larry Jackson, like Hunter RedDay, takes a sense of identity from the land where he lives.

Native North American Indians

BE ENRICHED BY OTHERS

Instead, says Larry, we each need to know who we are as we face the world. "You need to carry your identity with you. Then you won't be threatened by others' opinions. Differences can be interesting. Everyone brings something to the table. We can embrace our differences because they enrich us."

Hunter RedDay says something very similar. "It gets boring hanging out with people who are all the same. Why should we only listen to one kind of music? Why should we sing only one kind of song? Why should there be just one kind of human?"

Hunter believes that while humans have done cruel and terrible things to each other, humans can also do amazing things when they work together. "It's like we're a big tree that never stops growing," he says. "We each have our own branch to grow. We all have different jobs, different gifts— but together, they just make the tree grow faster, stronger, taller. Once you get it started, there's no stopping it. It just keeps growing."

Larry believes that those who live in poverty are part of that same growing tree. "We learn from need," he says. "We are enriched by the needs of others. We are taught by our own needs. This is what will one day make us all truly rich. We can't all live in mansions. If we do, we will destroy the Earth. Greed is not sustainable. We must be willing to learn from those who have nothing."

Hunter RedDay agrees. "We are here to learn from one another," he says. "We are all one, connected to the Earth. What hurts you, hurts me. What hurts the Earth, hurts us all. And it works the other way around too. What makes me better, will make you better. What heals the Earth, heals us. What heals us, helps heal the planet."

He stops talking for a moment and hums a Bob Marley song, "One Love," then adds, "Like Bob said, 'Let's get together.' We are all relatives, if you trace the DNA back far enough. White, black, Native—we're all human. We all have the same stories to tell. We're all God's children. But we're fragile. We need to realize just how fragile each other is. We're not like stones that can be banged around. We have to protect each other."

USE YOUR TALENTS

Hunter also believes the each of us have God-given gifts we can use to make the world a better place. "Use who you are, who you really are, to change the world. Use your flesh-and-blood talent. Stay true to yourself and your gifts. Follow your passion. Follow your heart. It will show you new doors to open."

Hunter knows from experience that living a creative life isn't always easy. "Sometimes," he says, "it will seem like you're starving. Maybe your body is literally hungry because you don't have enough to eat. Maybe it's your mind or your heart that's starving. But you can use even your hunger to fuel your creativity. If you're angry and frustrated, use that too! It's even okay if you feel like you're struggling and getting nowhere. Just keep playing your music, writing your

Prejudice Starts Inside

Sociologists have found that people who are prejudiced toward one group of people also tend to be prejudiced toward other groups. In a study done in 1946, people were asked about their attitudes concerning a variety of ethnic groups, including Danireans, Pirraneans, and Wallonians. The study found that people who were prejudiced toward blacks and Jews also distrusted these other three groups. The catch is that Danireans, Pirraneans, and Wallonians didn't exist! This suggests that prejudice's existence may be rooted within the person who feels prejudice rather than in the group that is feared and hated.

More Ways to Fight Prejudice

Here are some ways experts suggest you can fight prejudice when you find it inside yourself:

- Learn more about groups of people who are different from you. Read books about their history; read fiction that allows you to walk in their shoes in your imagination; watch movies that portray them accurately.

- Get to know people who are different from you. Practice being a good listener, focusing on what they have to say rather than on your own opinions and experiences. Ask about others' backgrounds and family stories.

- Practice compassion. Imagine what it would feel like to be someone who is different from you. Your imagination is a powerful tool you can use to make the world better!

- Be aware of the words you use. Avoid remarks that are based on stereotypes and challenge those made by others.

- Speak out against jokes and slurs that target people or groups. It is not enough to refuse to laugh; silence sends a message that you are in agreement.

- Volunteer to work with agencies that fight prejudice or that work on behalf of minorities in your community.
- Write letters to your newspaper, speaking out against discrimination in your community.
- Attend local cultural events.
- Eat at ethnic restaurants. Talk to the owners and staff while you're there.

Attending a powwow is a great way to experience some of the color and fun of Native culture.

Hunter RedDay's daughter is the face of the future. Hunter is working hard to ensure that the world she inherits is a better one.

words, singing your song, painting your art. Have faith. God gave you your gift for a reason. Your job is to use that gift, no matter what. It's what will lead you past prejudice inside yourself. It will open up new doors inside you. And it will also make new doors out there in the world, new doors for other people to go through."

We don't have to accept prejudice. As Mahatma Gandhi said, "Be the change you wish to see in the world."

"Let's do something new and different," is what Hunter says. "Together. Let's bake a brand new pie."

"Be willing to be a tool," is how Larry Jackson puts it. "The tool that builds something new. That teaches others. That changes the world."

"There's always hope for something better ahead." This is what Hunter RedDay believes with all his heart. "And it's never too late to change."

FIND OUT MORE

In Books

Brown, Dee. *Bury My Heart at Wounded Knee: An Indian History of the American West.* New York: Holt, 2007.

Dalton, C. H. *A Practical Guide to Racism.* New York: Gotham, 2008.

Dickason, Olive and David T. McNab. *Canada's First Nations: A History of Founding Peoples from Earliest Times.* New York: Oxford University Press, 2009.

Pritzker, Barry. *A Native American Encyclopedia: History, Culture, and Peoples.* New York: Oxford University Press, 2000.

Rattansi, Alan. *Racism: A Very Short Introduction.* New York: Oxford University Press, 2007.

On the Internet

101 WAYS TO COMBAT PREJUDICE
www.uen.org/utahlink/tours/tourFames.cgi?tour_id=15150

CANADA'S FIRST NATIONS
www.ucalgary.ca/applied_history/tutor/firstnations/

NAVAJO NATION HISTORY
www.navajo-nsn.gov/history.htm

YAVAPAI-APACHE NATION
www.yavapai-apache.org

GLOSSARY

advocate: Someone who speaks up on another's behalf.

commemoration: A ceremony or other event held in memory of some person or historical event.

commodities: Things that can be bought and sold.

culture: The art, language, beliefs, and ways of doing things that make a group of people unique.

elitism: The belief that certain groups of people deserve better treatment than others.

genocide: The deliberate killing of a large group of people.

homogenous: All the same.

immunity: The ability to resist germs.

interred: Held prisoner.

mentor: An advisor or teacher.

minorities: Groups that are smaller in number than the larger group to which they belong.

optimism: Confidence in the future.

oversimplification: The process of making something complicated too simple.

passion: Strong and powerful motivation.

proactive: Controlling a situation by causing something to happen rather than responding to events after they've already happened.

reservations: Land set aside by the government for Native groups.

sociologists: People who study the way groups of humans behave.

sovereign: Having the authority to govern oneself.

traditions: Ways of doing things and believing that have been handed down from generation to generation.

INDEX

BIBLIOGRAPHY

Farley, John E. *Majority-Minority Relations,* 5th ed. Upper Saddle River, N.J.: Prentice Hall, 2005.

Glenn, Edna, John R. Wunder, Willard Hughes Rollings, and C. L. Martin, eds. *Hopi Nation: Essays on Indigenous Art, Culture, History, and Law.* Digital Commons, digitalcommons.unl.edu/hopination, 2006.

Jackson, Larry. Personal communication. January 22, 2011.

RedDay, Hunter. Personal communication. January 23, 2011.

Yavapai-Apache Nation. "Exodus." www.yavapai-apache.org/culture.htm

PICTURE CREDITS

ABOUT THE AUTHOR

Ellyn Sanna is the author of hundreds of books for children, young adults, and adults. She has also worked for many years as an editor and small-business owner.

64